AF887474

What Our Readers Have Said...

"Although I consider myself a seasoned sales professional, it is helpful to have past learning's refreshed. The books were also beneficial because of the information concerning 'trends' in the sales relationship. The sales process should be viewed as dynamic since business relationships change regularly."

•

"For the particular business I am in and the type of sales calls I have, I find that the books in the Pinpoint Sales Training Series are very often applicable to how I conduct business. I would recommend them to other sales people, just not ones that are in my industry."

•

"These books provide very good concepts. It fits in well with the Bell Leadership training program that I attended in November."

•

"I use this material in these books and apply it to my customers and other employees I work with."

•

"I would like to know other topics. Is there anything on Production Management or Consultative Selling or Time Management?"

•

"These books are great tools that should be used as guidelines for our everyday

supervisory practices. You need to take the time to do a short self-evaluation when reading them."

•

"The Pinpoint Training Series delivers information that could be used in a lot different areas."

•

"I like this because I can take them with me to read at a convenient time. I feel the little time I have to spend in the office is best use on activities that directly relate to revenue opportunities. I like the short amount of time it takes to keep up with these."

•

"I prefer the self-study approach; it fits in with my schedule."

•

"My thought is that the real value of these books comes into effect when doing the action plans."

•

"Short and sweet. These books are easy to comprehend."

•

"I have enjoyed reading these books. They are relevant to today's work environment and the ongoing change in the way we manage our workforce."

•

"I do feel that these books have been very helpful to me at my job."

•

"I think a lot of the recommendations in these books are very useful, and can be applicable to everyday situations. If nothing else, it's a good reference guide to fall back upon if a situation arises in the future."

•

"These books are relevant to today's work environment and the ongoing change in the way we manage our workforce."

•

Sales Negotiations

Pinpoint Sales Skill Development Training Series

TIMOTHY F. BEDNARZ

MAJORIUM
BUSINESS PRESS

Pinpoint Sales Skill Development Training Series
"Sales Negotiations"
Timothy F. Bednarz

Graphic design: Monika Pawlak

Majorium Business Press
2025 Main Street
Stevens Point, WI 54481
715.342.1018 • 800.654.4935

ISBN 978-1-882181-74-2

Printed in the United States of America

Introduction

The Pinpoint Sales Skill Development Training Series is designed for targeted training and education regarding increased improvement in a specific skill or competency.

Each book within this series is designed to be easy to use, understand and apply to your job. It can be used as a basis for training individuals, as a discussion guide or as a personal training tool.

Each chapter within this book discusses a specific concept. When you have completed all eight chapters you should have a 360° perspective of the topic.

Additionally, each chapter is divided into specific sections:

- The first section provides you with an overview of the topic
- The Implications section discusses why the concept is important, and why it is important to learn and apply.
- The Strategies, Tips & Techniques to Apply section teaches how to use and apply the particular concept to your work.
- The Points to Ponder section gives you something to think about or to be discussed with a group setting. These are questions not meant to be immediately answered, but to be pondered over time.
- The Training Activity section provides you with the tools to transfer what you have learned to your job. It is designed to help create an action plan to effectively apply the concept.

Each of the topics in this series is time-tested and proven in the marketplace. They have been used by thousands of employees as training tools. Many of the users have commented that what made these books valuable, was the ability to refer to them when a problem surfaced. They indicated that they remembered reading about the exact problem. They referred back to these books and found an appropriate solution.

You will find them equally valuable as a resource in your professional development library.

Table of Contents

LEARNING OBJECTIVES:

- To understand the basic theory behind effective negotiating.
- To understand the elements and structure of negotiating.
- To use effective negotiating skills, tactics and strategies.
- To handle barriers to effective negotiating.

1

The Goals of Effective Negotiations

When salespeople think about negotiating a sales agreement, they often only consider the immediate contract itself without regard for the ramifications and implications of the agreement over time. Effective negotiating strategies have specific goals that form the foundation of all future customer relationships.

IMPLICATIONS — WHAT THIS MEANS TO YOU

Salespeople have the tendency to focus on the sale at the expense of the implications of the agreement, including customer relationship and retention issues. Many feel their responsibility ends once the sale is finalized. As more companies focus on the increased retention of their customers, salespeople must have specific goals that achieve more than the sale.

The negotiation of a sales contract must be considered the starting point of a sustainable customer relationship rather than an end in itself. Specific goals must be obtained outside of the particulars of the sale to ensure that good will and trust are developed as a result of the negotiations.

STRATEGIES, TIPS & TECHNIQUES TO APPLY

The goal of effective negotiations goes beyond reaching an agreement that results in a sale. Not all sales or agreements are equal. Each negotiated agreement has ramifications, consequences and implications. Effective negotiators manage and control all aspects of an agreement with an eye toward the future relationship with the customer. Factors to consider include:

Is It Fair?

"Fairness" is clearly a subjective term when discussing negotiations. A negotiated agreement is considered fair when both parties agree to it. However, there are circumstances where one party can assert their advantage and power over the other to reach an agreement.

For example, a customer may require a product or service by a specific date and is not in a position to negotiate the terms and price. Consequently, the salesperson may have received a premium price for his or her product or service. The agreement may be fair under the circumstances, but the customer may harbor ill feelings over being taken advantage of when no other options were available to them. When the opportunity arises, they will quickly switch to another potentially more equitable supplier.

In other circumstances, the customer may take advantage of a company or salesperson that clearly needs the business. In this case, the product or service may have been sold with little or no profit margin. The company will not be able to remain in business and sustain the account under these circumstances.

Salespeople must consider the long-term consequences of an agreement and consider what is both needed and fair to all parties.

Does It Deliver Value?

Customers buy solutions, not products or services. Packaged in the solution they are buying is the value that defines their satisfaction. Often in the midst of heated negotiations, both parties focus on their positions rather than on their interests. An effectively negotiated agreement focuses on the interests of both parties. This ensures that the agreement focuses on the customer's solutions, his or her expectations and the anticipated value.

Was Trust Established?

Salespeople must be concerned with the long-term consequences of negotiations to ensure that trust is established and sustained with the customer. If customers feel they were betrayed or manipulated during negotiations, salespeople will see their trust and credibility suffer.

Some of the goals of an effectively negotiated agreement are to build trust and credibility with the customer.

Was Good Will Promoted?

The major obstacle in most negotiations is emotion and not the issues. Intense negotiations can be emotionally draining for both parties. Salespeople must make sure that emotions remain in check and that there are no ill feelings created from intense and heated negotiations.

The key is to maintain control of emotions and to provide the customer with a sense that they have won the negotiations.

Was It Beneficial to Both Parties?

Effectively negotiated agreements are win-win propositions and built on the commonality between both parties. Only when buyer and seller both benefit from an agreement can a long-term relationship be built and established. If only one party benefits from the agreement, good will is undermined and ill feelings arise over the perceived unfairness of the agreement.

Is It Sustainable Over Time?

Nothing is achieved through the negotiations if the agreement is unsustainable. Agreements must stress the future cooperative behaviors between both parties. Salespeople must ensure that all misunderstandings are clarified and that all unspoken and non-negotiated issues and expectations are brought into the open and resolved. This avoids any potential future conflicts.

POINTS TO PONDER — SOMETHING TO THINK ABOUT

1. Have you experienced a negotiation that was unfair to either a customer or yourself? What was the result?
2. Have you built long-lasting sales relationships on win-win negotiations? If so, what particular methods did you use? If not, what can you do to change your approach?

TRAINING ACTIVITY — APPLICATION & ACTION PLAN

1. Identify a current sales agreement that you are negotiating or one that you recently completed.
2. Evaluate the effectiveness of your negotiating skills by determining:
    - Whether the agreement is fair to both parties.
    - The value the agreement delivers.
    - Whether trust is established with the customer.
    - If good will is developed with the customer.
    - Is the agreement is beneficial to both parties?
    - Is it sustainable over time?

2

Factors That Directly Impact Effective Negotiations

The probability of a successful negotiation is affected by the customer's perception of the relative strength of the salesperson's position. A number of variables come into play that can change daily according to how salespeople feel about themselves and how outside events impact their personal moods, feelings and attitudes.

A salesperson's perceived position of strength or weakness can change throughout the course of negotiations. The astute negotiator understands what can impact their position and how they can control it.

IMPLICATIONS — WHAT THIS MEANS TO YOU

Salespeople need to appreciate that negotiating a sale is something that cannot be undertaken without thought and preparation. There are a number of variables that have definite impacts on the success or failure of negotiations; some are clearly defined and delineated, while others are communicated nonverbally and affected by the salesperson's demeanor, beliefs and attitude.

Effective negotiating is not only impacted by a salesperson's skill level. His or her attitude, state of mind, self-esteem and a host of ever-changing variables will also impact a given negotiating session. When salespeople negotiate with a customer, their entire focus must be on the negotiations. Anything that blurs their focus diminishes their ability to effectively negotiate the sale.

STRATEGIES, TIPS & TECHNIQUES TO APPLY

The effectiveness of a salesperson's negotiating skills is impacted by five critical success factors. Salespeople must be aware how each impacts their negotiating position and the importance of each in the negotiating process.

Expectations

All negotiations are impacted by the expectations the buyer and seller bring to the table. Research studies have demonstrated that salespeople who expect to get what they want from the negotiations will get more. The firmness of the salesperson's belief in their position reduces the customer's expectations.

The customer's expectations are impacted and the salesperson's position is diminished when the salesperson gives up too much too fast. It is the customer's feelings about a concession in negotiations that counts, and they will feel little was received when so much is immediately conceded to them.

This dynamic presents a problem for the salesperson who views all negotiations from the perspective of price alone. Many will immediately make price concessions at the first sign of customer resistance. When salespeople offer concessions in negotiating, making each seem as important as possible keeps the customer's expectations in line. Salespeople who have a feeling of success gain negotiating power by influencing and controlling the customer's expectations.

Options

Before negotiations are initiated, salespeople prepare themselves by developing a number of negotiation options or positions to use when an impasse is reached or the customer does not agree to a specific position. These options are "what-if" scenarios that can be developed so that the salesperson can quickly shift tactics if the customer doesn't agree to the first. These scenarios—different product options, changes in terms and conditions, etc.—are designed to meet the customer's needs without surrendering substantial concessions.

Salespeople should also set their negotiating ranges. They should have a maximum and minimum position firmly established that keeps all of their options and possible concessions within these parameters. As the outcome of any negotiation is substantially affected by the pattern of concessions, salespeople should know in advance the allowances they are prepared to make and the order in which they will be made. Ideally, concessions should be made in small and diminishing increments. Research has shown that salespeople should avoid at all costs making the first major concession. This will have a dramatic impact on the outcome of the negotiations.

Power

Power is the result of what customers perceive the salesperson can do to meet their needs. There are three key factors that impact a salesperson's power in negotiations:

> *Need* – Nothing undermines a salesperson's negotiating position more than an openly expressed or demonstrated need for the sale. The customer will always do what is best for him or herself, and if they sense a salesperson's need for the order or perceive a sense of desperation, it will be used against them. Conversely, the salesperson who senses a customer's strong need for his or her product or service is in a more favorable position to hold firm during negotiations. Either party can increase their negotiating power by creating a perception that there are other options available to them.
>
> *Urgency* – The urgency to solve a problem or meet a deadline affects the negotiating power of each party. Without a sense of urgency, the customer has the power: there is no compelling reason for them to move the negotiations forward in a timely fashion. They are able to use time to positively impact their position.
>
> Salespeople are often able to develop a sense of urgency by creating artificial deadlines on quotes and proposals that might include favorable concessions if the customer acts by a specific date.

Information – The key to power in negotiations is superior customer knowledge. Effective negotiating skills demand that salespeople carefully listen to the customer's position and clearly determine what they want and expect from the negotiations. During active negotiations salespeople must get as much information as possible while giving as little as they can to reveal their position. Salespeople should not assume that the customer knows their weaknesses. This only lowers their own expectations and diminishes their negotiating power.

Communication – Open and active communication is essential in negotiations. Salespeople must solve issues so that they remain resolved. They have nothing if the agreement is not lasting. Issues that remain unspoken and un-negotiated will result in conflict. This is especially true with undefined customer expectations.

While during negotiations it is important for salespeople to develop a record of honesty and integrity in order to build trust and rapport with the customer, openness must be balanced with common sense. Too often salespeople diminish their position and undermine the negotiations by telling the customer too much about the deficiencies of their company and product.

POINTS TO PONDER – SOMETHING TO THINK ABOUT

1. Did you understand how the five critical factors impacted your negotiations in the past?
2. Do you see ways to strengthen your negotiating position in the future?

TRAINING ACTIVITY – APPLICATION & ACTION PLAN

1. Select a customer with whom you are about to enter into sales negotiations.

2. Identify the key success criteria that you need to positively impact the negotiations:
    a. Identify your expectations of the negotiations and those of the customer.
    b. Develop a list of "what if" scenarios in order to create alternative positions.
    c. Define your negotiating parameters including a list of diminishing concessions you are prepared to make.
    d. Determine your position of negotiating power from the issues of need, urgency and information.
    e. Define your communications goals and style to be used during the negotiations.
3. Examine whether there are factors that weaken your position and what you need to do to offset these and strengthen your overall negotiating position.

3

Avoiding the Major Pitfalls of Negotiating

The novice negotiator or one who has developed ineffective negotiating skills falls into a number of traps and pitfalls that can negatively affect the outcome of the negotiations and sale. Most of these common pitfalls can be avoided when salespeople are aware of them and trained in how to avoid them.

IMPLICATIONS — WHAT THIS MEANS TO YOU

Salespeople should not take negotiations lightly. The problem with many salespeople is that they approach a negotiating session in a cavalier manner. Rather than properly prepare themselves, they tend to "wing it" and assume that it is business as usual.

Effective negotiating skills can have a dramatic impact on salespeople's success and the size of their commission checks. Research has demonstrated that ineffective negotiators make more concessions and sell at lower price and profit levels than salespeople who have mastered and honed their negotiating skills. Additionally, effective salespeople are able to close more sales, and close them quicker, thus maximizing the use of their time.

STRATEGIES, TIPS & TECHNIQUES TO APPLY

There are a number of common pitfalls and traps that salespeople fall into when negotiating a sales contract. These include:

Preparation

Many salespeople are not adequately prepared to effectively negotiate a sales agreement. Many do undertake some form of preparation; however, outside of reviewing the sales proposal, they do not prepare to maximize results.

Adequate preparation includes outlining the objectives of the negotiations, detailing the issues and positions to be taken, fully understanding the buyer's needs and perspectives, determining the negotiating climate and developing specific strategies and alternative strategies if the initial approach does not work.

Attitude

A salesperson's negative attitudes, feelings and expectations can be a major liability when entering into negotiations. Poor self-image, low self-esteem and low expectations can lead to the assumption that they have less negotiating power than they actual do.

Salespeople must mentally prepare themselves when entering a sales negotiation. They must understand that their beliefs and attitudes will significantly affect negotiations. They must take the time to build their expectations and self-esteem before they enter into a negotiating session.

Negotiating Philosophy

Salespeople will often utilize an inappropriate negotiating style. A personal negotiating philosophy is closely linked to the personal goals and focus of the salesperson. Those with a sole focus on the sale and the sale alone can have a win/lose philosophy since they are only viewing negotiations from the standpoint of how they impact their commission and not in terms of the good of the customer. This perspective is guaranteed to increase friction and tension during negotiations since both parties are at odds with one another. Rather, salespeople should develop a win/win philosophy that focuses both parties on the accomplishment of common goals with a balanced solution.

Negotiating Style

The salesperson's negotiating style is quite different than their sales style. The customer or prospect has essentially been sold and is committed to the purchase of a specific product or service. The purpose of the negotiations is to then review all of the available options and arrive at a solution that is agreeable to both parties.

The use of manipulative negotiating tactics will only have a negative impact. Most buyers are increasingly skilled and trained in effective negotiating techniques. The fact that they are highly resistant to manipulative tactics increases barriers to the successful negotiation of a contract.

Emotional State

Salespeople who fail to pay attention to the buyer's negotiating state stumble into a common pitfall. Negotiating contracts involves many issues and positions that place both parties in conflict. The objective of negotiations is to resolve those conflicts, but talks can become heated as buyers grow emotional about specific issues and concerns. Salespeople who fail to monitor the emotional states of the buyer and keep their emotions in check can discover that the negotiations often become deadlocked to the point that the sale is ultimately lost.

Communication Skills

Effective negotiations demand superior communication skills. While listening skills are essential in selling, they are critical during negotiations. Salespeople must carefully listen to and interpret what is actually being said, since buyers will often mask or hide their true feelings to protect their position and negotiating power. Additionally, salespeople must be careful in the words they choose and the phrases they use because of the meanings they are transmitting.

Ineffective listening skills and the careless use of words and language can have a definite impact on negotiations. Once again, this is a common pitfall encountered by many salespeople.

POINTS TO PONDER — SOMETHING TO THINK ABOUT

1. Have you personally encountered some of the common negotiating traps and pitfalls described above?
2. Can you think of any additional traps and pitfalls you personally encountered?

TRAINING ACTIVITY — APPLICATION & ACTION PLAN

1. Analyze your personal negotiating skills to determine if you are falling into common traps and pitfalls:
    a. Determine the degree of preparation you take before a negotiating session. Identify all of the areas you prepare, including:
        - An outline of negotiating objectives and issues and positions to be taken
        - Whether or not you fully understand the buyer's needs and perspectives, determine the negotiating climate and develop specific strategies and alternative strategies if the initial strategies do not work.

    b. Analyze your personal attitudes including self-image, self-esteem and expectations.
    c. Determine your personal negotiating style.
    d. Identify your negotiating philosophy.
    e. Decide whether you monitor your buyer's emotional states and

keep your emotions in check.

f. Determine your communication skills.

2. Based upon your findings, identify the areas that you need to work on and improve.
3. Develop strategies to master and hone your skills to avoid common negotiating pitfalls and traps.

4

Correcting Problems During Current Sales Negotiations

When salespeople learn new skills, it is easy to apply them to the next situation that arises, but what can they do when they are deadlocked or in the midst of current negotiations? There are strategies that salespeople can use to reassess and reestablish their negotiating positions and successfully recover from problematic negotiations.

IMPLICATIONS — WHAT THIS MEANS TO YOU

Many negotiating problems stem from inadequate preparation and understanding that creates a situation that deadlocks the negotiations or places the salesperson in an unacceptable position. Left uncorrected, the salesperson can be forced to surrender valuable concessions and profitability that are essential to the existence of their company.

It is important for salespeople to appreciate that if they enter into negotiations unprepared or experience a deadlock, there are strategies and steps that can be taken to correct the problems and reestablish a stronger position. While the salesperson is still at a disadvantage, they can recover.

STRATEGIES, TIPS & TECHNIQUES TO APPLY

When salespeople are in the midst of sales negotiations and experience problems and possible deadlock or if they are just improving their negotiating skills and wish to apply them to current negotiations, the following steps can be taken:

Examine the Objectives

The objectives are the desired results that both salespeople and customers wish to achieve. When salespeople are familiar with both sets of objectives, they can identify the desired results that both parties agree upon and those that are resulting in conflict. The salesperson can easily rate the importance and priority of each specific objective. This provides them with a foundation for the negotiations. Often salespeople fail to do this and have no solid basis to negotiate. By examining the objective of the negotiations, they can reestablish a foundation and move forward from that point.

Review Positions and Issues

Salespeople need to identify all of the issues that are being discussed from both sides' perspectives. Once the issues are ascertained, they need to identify the position of each party on the issue, the importance of that issue and whether both parties are in conflict or agreement on it.

Review the Needs

All individuals are motivated by specific needs. These needs can be expressed as either company or personal necessities. In most sales negotiations, both company and personal needs are involved. Salespeople must identify these needs during the sales process and rank their importance.

Determine Strategies to Move Negotiations Forward

Once the salesperson has identified the customer's needs and motivations, strategies must be developed to meet those needs and move the negotiations forward. As strategies are developed, salespeople should rate their effectiveness in meeting the customer's requirements.

Review Negotiating Philosophy

While in sales negotiations—especially if they are deadlocked—salespeople must review and assess their personal negotiating philosophy. Philosophies other than a win/win approach can be causing the deadlock and producing a negative negotiating climate.

Review the Negotiating Climate

Salespeople must take a moment to view their negotiating philosophy from the customer's perspective. If it does not create a positive negotiating climate it must be changed. Additionally, salespeople must determine what, if anything, is changing the negotiating climate. Anything that negatively impacts the climate must be identified and addressed, as the more positive customers feel about the salesperson's approach, the more likely his or her solutions and positions will be accepted.

Reassess Negotiating Strategies

Once salespeople have reassessed the status of their existing negotiations, they are able to develop new strategies based upon their evaluation. When developing new strategies, salespeople must avoid concentrating on individual gains and pay attention to the effect strategies will have on the climate, their negotiating philosophy and overall goals.

POINTS TO PONDER – SOMETHING TO THINK ABOUT

1. Have you experienced problems or deadlocks in negotiations that you did not know or understand how to recover from?
2. What strategies have you successfully employed to recover from a problematic or deadlocked negotiation?

TRAINING ACTIVITY — APPLICATION & ACTION PLAN

Identify a current negotiation that you are in the middle of. Before you move any further:

1. Identify the customer's and your own objectives. Look for areas of agreement and conflict. Rank their importance.
2. Review the issues and positions taken by yourself and your customer. Look for areas of conflict and agreement. Rank them in order of importance.
3. Review the customer's needs and motivations and identify strategies to meet those needs. Rank the strategies by their effectiveness in meeting the customer's needs.
4. Define your negotiating philosophy and its impact on the negotiating climate.
5. Identify anything that is negatively impacting the negotiating climate and determine how to eliminate it.
6. Based upon your findings, reassess your negotiating strategies and make adjustments where necessary.

5

Elements of Successful Negotiations

There are specific elements that encompass successful negotiations. Skilled negotiators are aware of these elements and develop the base of information they need before entering into negotiations. They know by taking the time and effort required, they increase the likelihood of success.

IMPLICATIONS — WHAT THIS MEANS TO YOU

The elements of sales negotiations are nothing more than a structure with which to gather the necessary data and information, form a foundation and develop a strategy around. Without the development and formation of these elements, salespeople do not have a roadmap to follow to achieve their goals and objectives.

In negotiations, information is power. Any salesperson who is not fully informed before entering into talks is unprepared to achieve a successful outcome. The salesperson who takes the time to develop the necessary information upon which to base his or her negotiations is more likely to reach a profitable and sustainable outcome.

STRATEGIES, TIPS & TECHNIQUES TO APPLY

All negotiations encompass the following list of elements. Salespeople must be aware of each element and be fully informed of each one of them before they enter into negotiations. Salespeople should also know that they cannot take a canned approach to negotiations. While all of the elements will remain the same, the particulars will change with each specific negotiation and also can change in the middle of individual negotiating sessions.

Subject

Salespeople often assume that the subject matter of a negotiation is an area that both parties agree to, but this is not always the case. The salesperson may be negotiating the sale of a product or service while the customer is gathering competitive information that they can leverage against an existing supplier. Salespeople should define with the customer what is to be negotiated. The initial step in preparing to negotiate is to determine whether the customer shares the salesperson's understanding of the subject. If both parties cannot agree upon what is to be negotiated, or whether a negotiation is even taking place, then salespeople need to proceed with caution.

Objectives

Salespeople must define the objectives of the negotiation. Objectives must be more specific than just making a sale. Many salespeople tend to limit their objectives and consequently close their minds to creative alternatives and options. The key to successful negotiations is creating options that enhance the potential of a successful outcome. When developing objectives, salespeople should keep them realistic and attainable within the scope of the negotiations.

Fact-Finding and Assumptions

Before sales negotiations can begin, salespeople should have developed as much information as possible about the needs, concerns, problems and issues of the customer. This should have been done throughout the selling process, but especially during the qualification phase.

Salespeople must not make assumptions about the customer when entering into negotiations. All facts are viewed through the lens of the salesperson's assumptions. When salespeople develop information prior to negotiations they must be careful to remain objective in their evaluations and deal with facts rather than opinions.

Salespeople should understand that the basis of fact-finding is to establish a foundation for successful negotiations. Agreement on the facts is more important than the facts themselves. Salespeople should understand that as they enter into negotiations there are going to be facts and data they are not aware of; there is no way to know everything in advance.

Issues and Positions

Objectives are the things salespeople want to achieve; positions are the stances the salesperson takes to achieve them. If salespeople can get the customer to agree with their position, they can easily reach a negotiated settlement. When the customer does not agree with the salesperson, the point of disagreement becomes part of the issues that must be agreed upon. Fact-finding will often identify areas of differences and issues that must be negotiated. Salespeople should be aware that locking themselves into a specific issue becomes a negotiating trap.

Needs

Successful salespeople are attuned to the customer's needs and motivations and seek to assess their relative importance. They then craft unique product solutions around the customer's needs.

Needs and their satisfaction are the common denominators in negotiations. If the customer didn't have any needs, there would be no motivation for negotiations. When entering into negotiations, salespeople must identify both parties' needs and prioritize them. For lasting results, both the salesperson and the customer must have their needs satisfied so that both have a stake in its continued success.

Climate

Every negotiation has a climate. More than any other element, the climate will affect the results of the negotiations. If the salesperson can control the climate, they are likely to control the negotiations.

Salespeople must understand that the climate in which they operate is fluid and continually changing, requiring their constant attention throughout the negotiations. They should appreciate that climate is the product of many variables that can shift the mood of negotiations and completely reverse at a moment's notice. Salespeople must be attuned to the nonverbal communications that transpire during negotiations. These are the key to a shift in mood and climate.

Strategies and Tactics

Strategies are the game plan determining the moves that the salesperson will make throughout the negotiations. Tactics are the short-term moves designed to implement the strategy.

The salesperson's negotiating philosophy influences his or her strategies and tactics. All sales negotiations should be based upon a win/win philosophy.

POINTS TO PONDER — SOMETHING TO THINK ABOUT

1. Do you include and recognize all elements of negotiations in your customer exchanges?
2. What has been the result when you ignored any one of the elements of negotiations?

TRAINING ACTIVITY — APPLICATION & ACTION PLAN

Develop a fact-finding system that you can use during the entire sales process, that has a focus on developing the information you need to conduct successful negotiations. This system must include comprehensive customer knowledge, necessary for building and sustaining the agreement. However, additional information should be developed to satisfy the elements of negotiations listed above.

6

Preparing for Negotiations

Most sales and sales negotiations are determined before the process even begins. The degree to which sales and negotiations are successful is determined by the amount of time spent preparing. Salespeople reacting and responding to demands without forethought and consideration will needlessly surrender key concessions and profitability.

IMPLICATIONS – WHAT THIS MEANS TO YOU

Preparation is the key to successful negotiations. Salespeople who fail to prepare and enter negotiations without considering all sides and viewpoints of an issue face the possibility of being completely surprised and put on the defensive.

Adequate preparation allows salespeople to maintain control of the negotiations and achieve their goals and objectives without sacrificing profitability and key concessions.

STRATEGIES, TIPS & TECHNIQUES TO APPLY

Successful negotiation requires careful forethought and planning. The best preparation strategies require the salesperson to map out the entire process—from both the customer's and their own perspective—from beginning to end. In this manner they can explore both sides of the issue, examine possible positions, objectives and strategies the customer may take and prepare appropriate countermoves. Instead of a reactionary and defensive negotiating posture, this is an anticipatory and proactive approach that allows the salesperson to achieve specific goals and objectives.

The following points should be mapped out in advance of negotiations:

Subject Matter

Both the salesperson and the customer should be in agreement on the subject matter of the negotiations. If both parties cannot agree upon this point, the negotiations cannot move forward. While this may appear self-evident, salespeople cannot assume that both parties are negotiating a sale. The customer may be only seeking information or shopping for the best option. There can be different reasons and motivations that both parties must agree upon.

Objectives

Salespeople must determine the maximum and minimum objectives that they are willing to accept and compare them to the maximum and minimum objectives of the customer. Additionally, they should be looking at ways that both parties can expand their objectives.

Fact-Finding

During negotiations, information is power. Salespeople enter negotiations with the information they have developed during the sales process. Once negotiations commence, the customer will limit any additional information they may be willing to provide. If the salesperson has properly qualified the customer, sufficient information should be available to make accurate assumptions. However, they should take time to identify any hidden assumptions they are also making that underlie their negotiating posture.

The salesperson should also identify both the assumptions and hidden assumptions that the customer may be making about him or her.

Issues

Salespeople should identify the points of agreement and disagreement between both parties and classify them as either major or minor issues.

Positions

Salespeople need to identify the stands that they intend to take on the issues as well as the customer's positions. This should clearly identify the negotiating climate and the salesperson's expectations of the negotiations. Fallback positions should be established by creating a number of "what-if" scenarios that identify and counter various positions that the customer may take.

Needs

The needs of both parties should be identified and prioritized. Successful salespeople will craft their negotiating strategies around the satisfaction of their customer's needs, often by expanding or identifying options they had not previously considered.

Climate

The issues, positions and needs of both parties should identify the negotiating climate the salesperson is developing. Salespeople should remember that if they control the climate, they control the negotiations. All factors should be considered and elements added to create a favorable negotiating climate.

Strategy

After mapping all of the elements detailed above, salespeople should be able to determine the overall plan they intend to use during the negotiations, including the moves they plan to take, when to take them and any countermoves and fallback positions that should be anticipated.

In this manner, salespeople should be able to effectively negotiate a successful sales agreement that meets the needs of both parties without sacrificing key concessions that can impact the sustainability of the sales relationship and the profitability of the business.

POINTS TO PONDER — SOMETHING TO THINK ABOUT

1. How much forethought do you put into your negotiation preparation? Could you benefit from more comprehensive negotiation planning?
2. Have you ever been involved in a negotiation that broke down? If so, what parts of the negotiation process did you fail to map out?

TRAINING ACTIVITY — APPLICATION & ACTION PLAN

Develop a map of a negotiating session you are about to enter in. Take the time to map out your side and the customer's side of the negotiations by considering the following points:

- Subject Matter
- Objectives
- Fact-Finding
- Issues
- Positions
- Needs
- Climate
- Strategy

7

Negotiating Tactics and Strategies

Negotiating strategies are the tools used by salespeople to change relationships. The overall purpose of successful negotiations is not to win the battle and the sale only to lose the long-term customer. Rather, negotiations are successful when things of value are exchanged by both parties and not appropriated by one side.

IMPLICATIONS — WHAT THIS MEANS TO YOU

Both parties involved in sales negotiations will employ a series of strategies and tactics to achieve their objectives. Each has specific purposes and consequences. Any strategy employing high-pressure and manipulative tactics can anger the other party, alter the complexion of the negotiations and change the overall climate.

The overall purpose of negotiations should be to win a customer for life rather than gain a short-term sale. If the stakes are high and one side feels that they have been shortchanged in the negotiations, long-term negative consequences will seriously erode the customer relationship. The point is to strike a balance between the needs of both parties to the satisfaction of each.

STRATEGIES, TIPS & TECHNIQUES TO APPLY

Negotiating strategies are the long-term moves that salespeople use to achieve their objectives, while tactics are the short-term maneuvers used to implement those strategies.

Salespeople should be prepared to change their tactics and strategies in response to the other party's reactions. They need to closely observe the body language and the content and meaning of what the other party is communicating. Additionally, they must be cognizant of the hidden meanings behind the responses made during negotiations.

Salespeople must also be aware of the feelings or environment created during the negotiating process. The things salespeople say, and how they say them, as well as their appearance and many other nonverbal factors create this climate. Salespeople can create a supportive climate or a negative and defensive climate that can undermine the entire negotiation.

There are a number of specific strategies that can be employed by either party during a sales negotiation. The most common strategies and tactics seen in sales negotiations include:

> *Forbearance* – This is the use of time to gain an advantage. One side may stall knowing that the other side has a pressing need.
>
> *Surprise* – Either side may introduce new facts, circumstances or variables that alter the balance of the negotiation, compelling the other side to assume a defensive posture.
>
> *Fait Accompli* – This is a strategy that either party may use. It is a posture of assuming that both parties have already agreed to the sale and the negotiations are a mere formality.
>
> *Apparent Withdrawal* – When conflicts arise, one side will give the impression that they are withdrawing from their position and that concessions or adjustments will be made, when in fact they are luring the other side into a false sense of security, because they fully intend to maintain their position.
>
> *Reversal* – When faced with pressure, one side or another backs away from their original position and completely reverses their stance.
>
> *Limits* – In this case, either party has set specific boundaries on their negotiating positions. They will remain flexible as long as they stay

within their prescribed limits. Once forced outside of their limits, they will hold firm to their position.

Feinting – Salespeople can put up a smokescreen to deceive the buyer into thinking they are going to receive something they're not.

Bracketing – Salespeople will set their prices above the desired sales level anticipating the buyer will negotiate for lower prices. The salesperson then proposes splitting the difference, which then brings them to the desired price.

Crossroads – When pressured to make concessions, salespeople agree to them only when the buyer meets all stipulated conditions that ultimately counter the original concession.

While these strategies and tactics are commonly encountered, many variations are seen in the marketplace. Even if salespeople do not use specific tactics and strategies, they should be aware that they exist and be familiar with them so that they can be easily recognized and addressed when encountered. When salespeople can recognize specific tactics and strategies employed by the customer, then it is relatively easy to successfully counter their moves.

POINTS TO PONDER – SOMETHING TO THINK ABOUT

1. Are you aware of the specific tactics or strategies used during sales negotiations?
2. Have you used high-risk tactics or strategies that impacted a negotiation, changing the climate and complexion?

TRAINING ACTIVITY – APPLICATION & ACTION PLAN

Determine the negotiating tactics and strategies that your normally employ.

1. Identify the specific tactic or strategy that describes it.

2. Determine your objective in using that tactic or strategy.
3. Identify the potential impact of that tactic or strategy on negotiations.
4. Define the risks involved in using that tactic or strategy.
5. If the tactic or strategy is high-risk, what alternatives can you use that makes the risk more acceptable?

8

Key Actions That Effect Negotiation Strategies

Salespeople must take a number of key actions to ensure that the sale progresses into successful negotiations and that they stay on top of a dynamic environment in which things can change in an instant. These are actions, tactics and strategies that ensure that the negotiations run smoothly and achieve the desired goals.

IMPLICATIONS – WHAT THIS MEANS TO YOU

Salespeople should understand that during negotiations everything remains fluid and flexible until an agreement is reached. This also means that once negotiations begin proposals, preliminary agreements and commitments are subject to change and are not final until the contract is signed.

In addition to flexible, salespeople must be vigilant for the changes in conditions and circumstances that can affect the final outcome and be prepared to make alterations and modifications to their negotiating position and documents—primarily their sales proposal, which is the basis of the negotiation.

STRATEGIES, TIPS & TECHNIQUES TO APPLY

Salespeople need to understand that plans for negotiations are worthless if the actual negotiation never takes place. If they appreciate the following factors, they will help ensure that they advance the sale to the negotiation stage:

No Proposal Is Ever Complete

No proposal is ever complete. As it represents a compromise based upon the limits of time and energy, there is always room for improvement.

The salesperson serves the interests of both parties when they review the proposal after it has been submitted. Requirements and needs may have been overlooked and other sections may require further clarification.

Never Be Afraid of Making Changes

During negotiations, conditions can change frequently. Salespeople should feel free to make adjustments and changes to their proposal as required. This is both proper and appropriate. In fact, salespeople should ask the customer whether the proposal is responsive to their needs and requirements and ask what can be done to clarify its content for them.

Consider the Type of Purchase

Salespeople should understand the type of purchase that is being made. If proposals are sought for a low-bid or advertised purchase, the lowest price obviously wins the contract.

If the purchase is being negotiated, it is permissible for the customer to inform the salesperson that his or her price is too high. In this process, it is also permissible for salespeople to change their proposal in response to a change in information, circumstances or conditions.

Monitor the Proposal

Salespeople should monitor the proposal after it is submitted through their additional contacts in the customer's business. Although it is not good business to discuss a proposal, many buyers do. By actively monitoring what is happening, they can gain insight and information that can assist them in the final negotiations.

Note Casual Comments

During negotiations, salespeople should pay particular attention to casual comments and nonverbal communication. These often unspoken positive indications can be as indicative of the customer's intent as firm statements.

Invest Expertise

When customers are relating product and service specifications early in the sales process, salespeople should bring any technical staff and expertise to bear on the process. This investment usually pays off later when the customer is making the final selection for several reasons. First, the salesperson and his or her company have demonstrated a genuine interest in and concern for the customer. Second, input regarding the development of specifications allows the salesperson to include particular details about his or her product that the competition may find difficult to meet.

Be Thoroughly Familiar with the Proposal

Salespeople should be thoroughly familiar with their proposal and have the expertise to explain and, where necessary, defend every point presented to the customer. Salespeople who are unable to do this will lose credibility and stature in the negotiating process. The best defense against any assaults on a proposal during negotiations is the ability to quickly and professionally draw from and present data.

Leverage Experience and Expertise

Salespeople know more about their products and cost structure than the customer. Experience and expertise are the differentiating factors in sales. Salespeople should leverage their expertise and experience during the negotiations to bring relevance to what is being presented and to clearly and concisely demonstrate the value they are capable of delivering.

POINTS TO PONDER — SOMETHING TO THINK ABOUT

1. How actively do you monitor your sales proposals once they have been submitted to the customer?
2. After submitting proposals to customers, have you modified and altered them to account for changing conditions and circumstances?

TRAINING ACTIVITY — APPLICATION & ACTION PLAN

1. Identify specific ways that you can leverage your experience and expertise during a sales negotiation.
2. Determine exactly what you bring to the negotiating table and how it can be used to a specific advantage.

About the Author

Timothy F. Bednarz, Ph.D. is CEO of the American Management Development Group, Inc. For over 20 years he has researched, designed and authored hundreds of learning and development programs used by Fortune 1000 companies.

He is also the author of *Great! What Makes Leaders Great. What They Did, How They Did It and What You Can Learn from It* (2011).

Speaking Availability

Timothy F. Bednarz, Ph.D. is available for speaking engagements for your next meeting or association event. He can be contacted at 800-654-4935 or by e-mail at timothy.bednarz@majorium.com.

Bulk Sales

Bulk sales of this book or any other titles available from Majorium Business Press. Inquiries can be directed to sales@majorium.com, or by phone at 800-6654-4935.

Quick Order Form

Fax orders: 715-342-1118. Send this form.

Telephone orders: Call 800-654-4935 toll-free. Have your credit card ready.

Email orders: sales@majorium.com

Postal orders: Majorium Business Press, 2025 Main Street, Stevens Point, WI 54481, USA.

Please send the following books:

____

____

____

____

Please send more FREE information on:

❑Catalog ❑Speaking/Seminars ❑Mailing Lists ❑Consulting

Name: ____________________________________

Address: __________________________________

City: ____________________ State: _____ Zip: __________

Telephone: ________________________________

Email address: ______________________________

Sales tax: Please add 5.5% for products shipped to Wisconsin addresses.

Shipping by air:

United States: $4.00 for first book and $2.00 for each additional product.

International: $9.00 for first book; $5.00 for each additional product (estimate).

Made in United States
Orlando, FL
04 November 2026

90202050R00028